TRUCK FULL
OF DUCKS

TRUCK FULL OF DUCKS

Ross Burach

scholastic inc.

Thanks for calling Truck Full of Ducks...
We'll be right there!

munch
munch
munch

OH NO! The directions!

Don't worry, ducks.
We'll find the customer!

Did you call for a truck full of ducks?

No, not me. I called for a mail truck.

Did you call for a truck full of ducks?

No, dude, not us. We called for an ice cream truck!

Who called for a truck full of ducks?

Did you call for a truck full of ducks?

Arrr! It wasn't me, matey. I called for a truck full of crackers . . . not quackers!

WHO CALLED FOR A TRUCK FULL OF DUCKS??

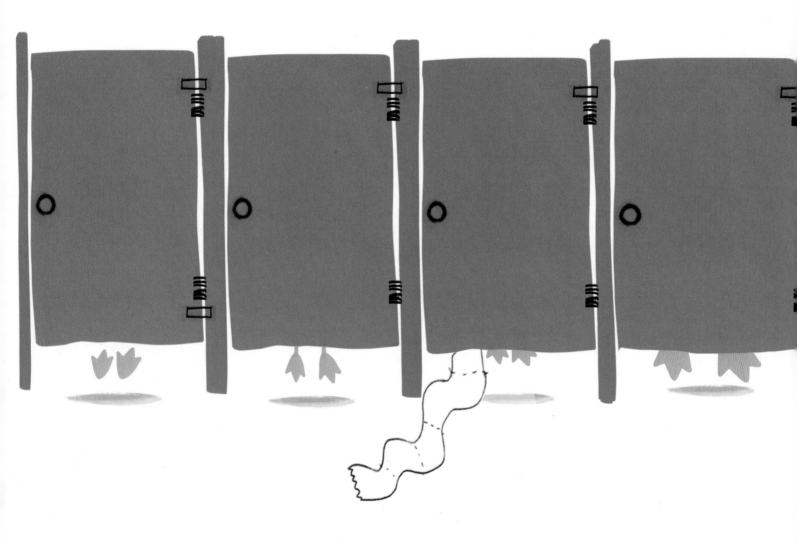

HURRY UP, ducks!

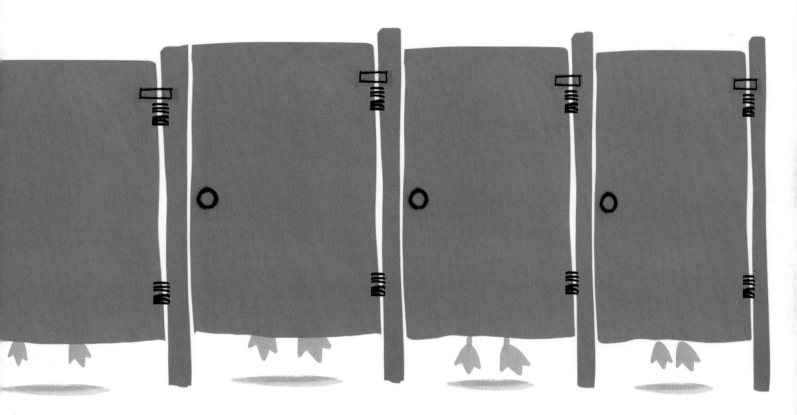

Back in the truck! The clock is ticking!

Did **YOU** call for a truck full of ducks?

AHHHH! NO! NO MORE DUCKS!
I called for a duck REMOVAL truck!

Okay, ducks. Out of the truck!
See, I told you not to worry.

. . . is over!
Time for my bath!

Thanks for calling Truck Full of Ducks . . .
We'll be right there!

To Tracy, Marijka, and Kait — one quacky crew! — R.B.

Ross Burach's drawings were created with pencil, crayon, acrylic paint, and digital coloring. · The text type was set in Loyola Pro Bold and Loyola Pro. · The display type was set in Chaloops Bold. · Production was overseen by Angie Chen. · Manufacturing was supervised by Shannon Rice. · The book was art directed by Marijka Kostiw, designed by Ross Burach and Marijka Kostiw, and edited by Tracy Mack.